WM. B. EERDMANS
PUBLISHING CO.
Grand Rapids, Michigan

MARSHALL PICKERING
CHRISTIAN since 1794 PUBLISHERS

SARAH
A woman whose dream came true
Retold by Marlee Alex
Illustrated by Charles Barat
© Copyright 1986 by Scandinavia
Publishing House, Nørregade 32, DK-1165 Copenhagen K.
English language edition first published 1987
through special arrangement with Scandinavia
jointly by W. B. Eerdmans Publishing Co.,
255 Jefferson Ave. S.E. Grand Rapids, Michigan 49503
and
Marshall Pickering, 3 Beggarwood Lane, Basingstoke,
Hants RG23 7LP, England
All rights reserved
Printed in Singapore
Eerdmans **ISBN 0-8028-5015-4**
Marshall **ISBN 0-551-014857**

Outstanding Women of the Bible

SARAH

A woman whose dream came true

Retold by Marlee Alex
Illustrated by Charles Barat

The Bible is the story of God's dealings with his people. This story is like a picture God painted for all the world to see. God wanted to show everyone, everywhere, how much he loves ordinary people, and how he can make wonderful things happen through ordinary lives.

Israel was the kind of nation whose laws and traditions gave men the leadership in government and family life. However, Israel's history is full of stories of women. Some of these women rose to become leaders. Others shaped and changed the life of their nation as they stayed in the background. These stories stress the unique influence that women can have on history.

In Israel, the influence of women might have been limited by the customs and laws of their country, or by personal things like the amount of money they had, the type of education, their husband's position, or the number of children in the family. But in these stories we meet woman after woman who, in spite of outward hindrances, was limited only by the degree of her faith in God or by the degree of her determination to use the gifts he gave her.

We hope this book will make you eager to be used by God, and help you to believe more than ever before that you can be all God made you to be.

William B. Eerdmans Publishing Company,
Grand Rapids, Michigan

Marshall Pickering
Basingstoke, England

3

S|arah!"

Abraham was still in the distance.
Sarah put her needlework aside and went
to the tent door. Abraham came running
with a big dust cloud at his heels.

"Sarah! Sarah, God spoke to me out in
the hills!" Abraham was out of breath.
"God said I am going to be a father
after all. He said our children will be a
blessing to the whole world. That means
it's not too late for us to have a baby. You
will be a mother, Sarah!"

Abraham paused for breath. He had run
all the way from the sloping mountainside
and followed the long dusty path back
home to his wife.

The tent was snuggled under a mighty
oak tree. Branches stretched out over
their fire and sleeping mats. This was not
the first time Abraham came home to
Sarah saying that God had spoken to him
and promised them a child. But a long
time had passed since the last time.

Sarah felt bubbly inside once again. "Oh, Abraham, I haven't given up hope for that child. And if anyone can recognize the voice of God, you can. I know you listen to God. I'm glad I married you."

Sarah and Abraham had been married many years, but no children had been born to make them the kind of family Sarah dreamed about. Not once had she watched her tummy grow with a baby. Not once had she ever felt tiny thumps and kicks from the inside. Sarah cried many times as month after month passed. She wanted to be a mother, but that seemed like something that happened only in fairy tales.

Sometimes Sarah daydreamed about it. She would dream about the "ga-ga" sounds of a baby at her breast or about a laughing child playing at her feet. Abraham knew what she was thinking about when he saw that faraway look on her face. But he could not make her dream come true. He felt sorry too. Often, he prayed about having a child as he walked in the hills with the herds of oxen and flocks of sheep.

On warm evenings, Sarah and Abraham slept side by side under the stars outside their tent. They loved to watch shooting stars fall across the black sky at bedtime. Once Sarah had tried to count the stars, but there were all too many of them. The stars became a dusty blur. Stardust seemed to fall into her eyes all too soon and she fell fast asleep.

6

Sarah and Abraham had once lived in a different country called Haran. One day Abraham came home and said, "We're leaving!"

"What, leaving?" Sarah asked.

"Yes, God told us to take a trip!"

"What do you want me to pack, winter clothes or summer clothes?"

Abraham's reply shocked Sarah: "Pack both," he announced. "We're leaving. We'll never come back to Haran."

So Sarah and Abraham left their family and friends behind. God had told them to go to the land of Canaan. Sarah sorted through all their clothes and furniture. She gave away everything they would not be needing. But she kept one thing that was too precious to leave behind. It was a secret.

"Maybe I will need this someday," she said to herself.

9

ow, under the mighty oak at Marah in Canaan, Sarah lifted the small box from its hiding place. Abraham was outside washing up. Sarah opened the box and took out one of the baby gowns folded inside. She had sewn the gowns herself. They were made of white linen, embroidered with colored thread and trimmed with lace. Sarah was glad she had brought them with her to Canaan. Now God had spoken again to Abraham about the child he had promised.

"I'm going to be needing these one day," she mused.

Abraham's voice broke her thoughts. "Sarah, we'll be moving on tomorrow," he said. "This isn't the place we're supposed to settle down."

Sarah was getting used to breaking camp and packing up. "Well, it will be nice when we do find the right place," she called back cheerfully.

Once again, they packed up and travelled southward. The long train of camels, donkeys, sheep, oxen and all the servants of Abraham made its way slowly through the hills of Canaan. They often stopped to rest. The animals were allowed to graze where the grass was high. The children of the servants splashed in cool streams and pools. Abraham and Sarah took time to worship God. God had called them to Canaan and they were certain he would guide them along the way.

But after weeks of travel the barrels of dried food they had brought along began to look empty. The fresh fruits they had eaten along the way became difficult to find. The green hills of Canaan turned rocky and dry. Abraham's servants began to complain. "We're getting hungry," they cried.

So Abraham had to make a decision. "Let's go east!" he told them. "I've heard there is plenty of food and water in the land of Egypt."

But there was one problem. Egypt was a strong country. Abraham was carrying lots of silver and gold with him. He was afraid the Egyptians would try to rob him. Perhaps they would even try to kill him. Abraham tried to think of ways to make friends with the Egyptians.

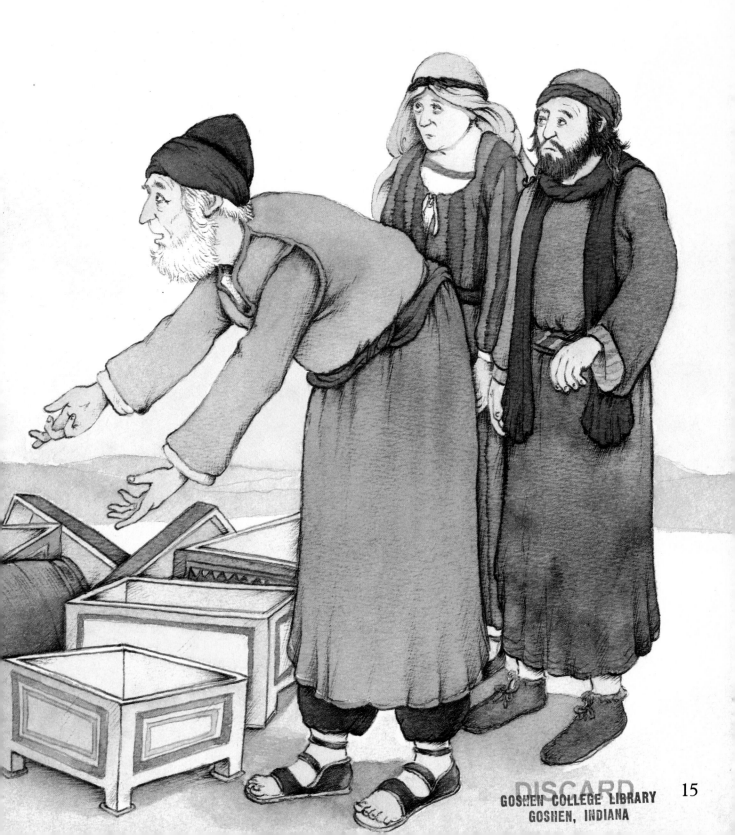

Sarah was riding on ahead of Abraham. She sat straight and tall on her camel. Her lovely silhouette against the blue sky gave Abraham an idea. Many other men had admired Sarah because she was very beautiful. Many times Abraham had seen them glance sidewards at her as she passed by in villages or watering places.

Abraham rode up beside Sarah. "Sarah, you are lovely," he said. "You are bound to be noticed by the men in Egypt. I've been worrying about something. The Egyptians might try to kill me in order to get you for a wife. If that happened then God would not be able to keep his promise to us. Sarah, I'm afraid.

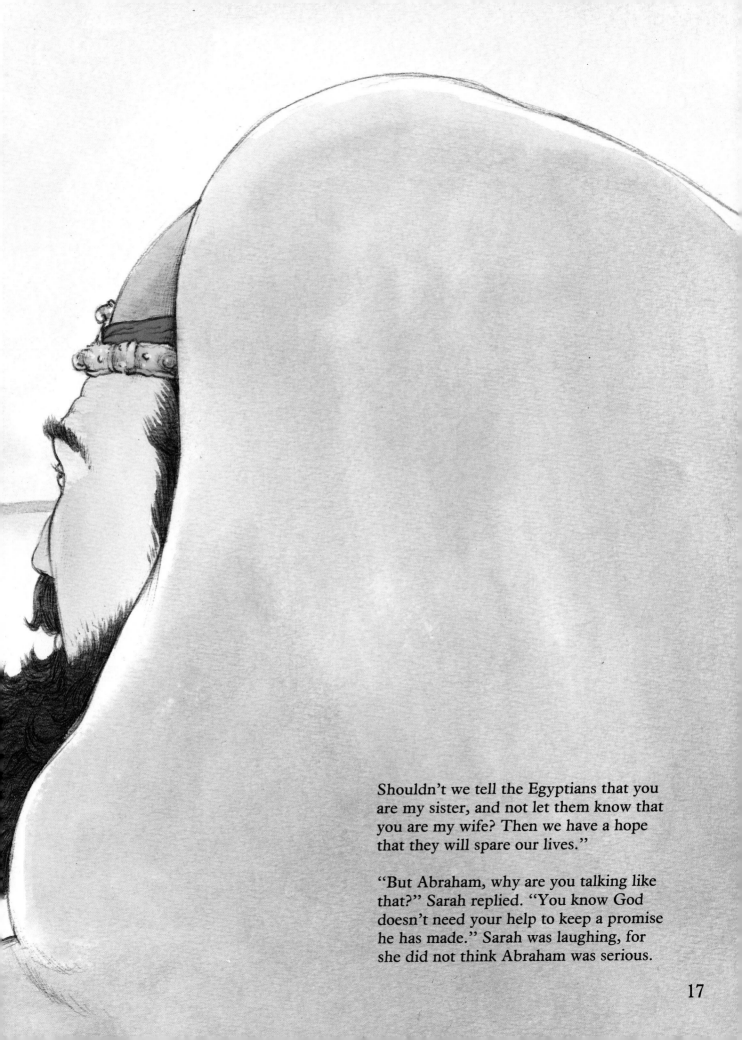

Shouldn't we tell the Egyptians that you
are my sister, and not let them know that
you are my wife? Then we have a hope
that they will spare our lives."

"But Abraham, why are you talking like
that?" Sarah replied. "You know God
doesn't need your help to keep a promise
he has made." Sarah was laughing, for
she did not think Abraham was serious.

The two of them rode on together in front of the camel train. But when they arrived in Egypt Sarah realized that what Abraham had predicted was true. Heads turned toward her as she rode through towns. The eyes of many a man looked into hers. Talk about her beauty flew from mouth to mouth. Eventually, even Pharaoh, the king of Egypt, heard about her. Pharaoh was a man who was used to getting whatever he wanted, and so he insisted on having Sarah as his wife.

Pharaoh's army rode out to the place where Abraham and Sarah had made camp. Abraham turned to Sarah with fear in his eyes. But Sarah jumped up and hurried out to meet them. She thought that they intended to kill Abraham. She spoke quietly with the soldiers and then rode away with them. Not one of them turned back after Abraham. He stared after them. He did not know what to think.

The next day several of the soldiers came riding back to Abraham's camp. "Now they are coming to kill me," he thought. But the soldiers were carrying treasure chests and leading herds of animals.

20

The soldiers rode up and laid the chests at Abraham's feet, bowing before him. "These gifts are from Pharaoh," they announced. "Pharaoh wishes to say thank you and to tell you he is pleased with Sarah." Then the soldiers rode away.

Abraham was stunned. He buried his face in his head scarf. He realized that Sarah must have told them that she was his sister anyway. Then Pharaoh would not have to kill Abraham to get her as a wife. Abraham felt sad and sorry. "God, help me get Sarah back," he prayed.

21

And God did! That day God sent a terrible sickness upon Pharaoh and upon everyone who lived in his house, except Sarah. That made Pharaoh realize that he had done something wrong by taking Sarah as his wife.

"Go back to your husband!" Pharaoh commanded Sarah. "And get out of Egypt with all your servants and animals. I never want to see you again."

Sarah ran back to Abraham as fast as she could. Abraham gathered his company and they all trooped quickly out of Egypt. Everyone was relieved to get back to Canaan again. They managed to find enough to eat, and God continued to tell Abraham that he would protect and bless them. God said he would give all the land of Canaan to their children.

But Abraham and Sarah still did not have a child. Ten years had passed since God had promised the first time. Abraham believed God's promise. He tried to assure Sarah that God meant to keep it.

One day Sarah admitted to Abraham, "How can I go on believing? God promised us we would have a son and as many grandsons as there are stars! How silly! There are more stars than I can count, but not once has my body ever given a hint that I can bear a child. And now I am too old to even dream of it!

"Here Abraham," she continued. Tears filled her eyes, but she fought them back. "You may take my servant, Hagar, as your wife.

She is young and lovely. Perhaps God will give you a son through her." With a heart full of sadness Sarah left the tent and hurried away to a distant well to fetch water. There she could be alone and cry out her tears before God himself.

Abraham was sorry when Sarah ran off. But he thought to himself, "Maybe Sarah is right." So he did what she had suggested. Abraham slept with Sarah's servant, Hagar, as if she was his wife. Before the end of a year Hagar gave birth to a baby boy. They named the baby Ishmael. Ishmael and his mother, Hagar, continued to live close to Abraham and Sarah and to serve them as year after year passed.

When Abraham and Sarah were almost 100 years old God spoke to Abraham once more. This time God made a special promise about Sarah. "The name Sarah means 'princess'," he said. "Sarah will be blessed like a princess. She will have children who will grow to be kings. Next year she will give birth to a son. You are to call him Isaac. That means 'laughter'. And I will give this land of Canaan to him and to his sons after him."

This time Abraham did not dare tell Sarah what God had said. He had enough trouble believing the promise himself! But one hot summer afternoon as he and Sarah were sitting in the shade beside their tent, three men came walking over the hills towards their camp. Abraham stepped out to welcome the men. He took a crock of water with him and called back to Sarah, "Go in and mix up a fresh batch of bread for our visitors."

As they approached the tent one of the men asked Abraham, "Where is your wife, Sarah?"

"In the tent," Abraham answered.

"This time next year, you and Sarah will have a baby boy!" another one of them exclaimed.

Sarah was standing inside the tent door, and heard what the man had said. She started to chuckle quietly as she thought to herself, "A ninety-one year old woman like me having a baby? Oh, no! God has had plenty of time, but now it's too late."

The third man's voice interrupted Sarah's thoughts. "Why is Sarah laughing?" he asked.

Sarah knew that he could not possibly have heard her. Suddenly she felt scared and excited at the same time.

The third man continued speaking. "You just wait and see. It will happen just like we said it would," he insisted.

There was a lump in Sarah's throat. She swallowed hard and whispered, "Oh, but I did not laugh." She peeked out of the tent door. The men were already heading down the dusty road. There was something different about them. Were they holy men? Prophets? God himself?

The months passed by and Sarah could not forget the men or what they had said. Sarah's face was tanned and wrinkled. Her back was crooked with age. Her shoulders were stooped. But now her stomach began to grow. It became bigger and rounder every day. Her long robes flared out in front and fell short of the ground. Everyone could plainly see that she was expecting a baby, but Sarah was almost afraid to believe it herself.

However, sure enough, within a few months' time, a healthy baby boy was born to Sarah and Abraham. Sarah's heart leapt with joy as she held up his soft little body. "God has made me laugh!" she told everyone. "And everyone who ever hears about this—that an old woman like me can have a child—will laugh with me and be happy!" Sarah's face looked young again and her dim eyes lit up with hope.

Sarah's impossible dream had come true at last. She learned that God always keeps His promises, and that he doesn't need anybody's help to do it. Sarah lived a long time after that and she watched Isaac, the child of her dreams, grow to become a man.